The Co-op Label

Marlene Wisto

Some of these poems appeared in *Pemmican, North Coast Review,
North Stone Review*, and *Seneca Review.*

ISBN 0-9765890-0-1

Printed and bound in Canada
Layout and design by Marlene Wisuri
Cover photograph by Marlene Wisuri
Back Cover, collection of the Carlton County Historical Society

Dovetailed Press LLC

*Dovetailed Press LLC
5263 North Shore Drive
Duluth, MN 55804
www.dovetailedpress.com*

The Co-op Label

Poems by Jim Johnson   Images by Marlene Wisuri

Dovetailed Press LLC
Duluth, Minnesota

Table of Contents

Being poetry, history, photography, this book is a co-operative venture. It bears *The Co-op Label* for your inspection. While Part I portrays immigration and the anti-immigration activities of 1918, Part II alludes to anti-communist sentiments of the 1950s. Although Part II was inspired in part by *The Co-operative Builder*, January and July 1943, issues, most of it is fiction. Part III hovers around the question—whether Co-operation is a remnant of the past or a seed of our future. This, we think, is a past that more and more needs reinvention.

This book is dedicated to immigrants
and co-operators everywhere.

Part One: Immigrants

We Are All Immigrants

I was born in this country.
My mother was born in the old country.
As I was born of my mother, I was born of the old country.
As she is an immigrant, I am an immigrant.
As I am an immigrant, we are all immigrants.
Together we are all crossing the land bridge, arm in arm.
Together we are all leg-ironed, ballast in a slave ship.
Together we are all sick with the fever in steerage,
    in the hold our bodies retching, folded in prayer.
We are all immigrants together. All our possessions in
    a single trunk.
The photographs of ancestors stained with olive oil.
Our longing cured with lutefisk.
Our *viilia* dried and, like our past, pressed between the
    pages of our Bible. And
in sacks of medicine: in muskrat skin: arrowroot, eagle down,
    and dried flowers.
Only a gold locket and a few seed potatoes in a pocket.
Our hopes already reduced by early winters, uncertain words,
    and drought.
Together we are crossing the barbed wire.
The stars arcing in the corners of our eyes.

At Kaleva Hall

They met every Tuesday evening. First the women met in the
women's room and men met in the men's room. Then they all
became people again and went upstairs to the great hall.

One time my grandmother took me with her. On stage there
was a man so old his hair was gray and thin as a wasp's nest in
the rafters of the old hay barn. I know now that barn wouldn't
last the weight of another winter. His hands shook as if a wind
had come up as he put on his glasses. Then, I will always
remember; he began to read.

In those days there was a sign: *This room is equipped with
Edison Electric Light. Do not attempt to light with a match.
Simply turn key by the door.* And it was as if his voice became
the voice of Edison and turned that key.

The men shut up.
The women stood so still. They all wore dark dresses from the
old country and *huivis* they made themselves draped over their
heads. Tears streamed down their cheeks. I asked my grandmother
why, why they were all so sad, but she said I wouldn't
understand: it was poetry.

Surprised By God Grandmother Turned To Spells

Driving all morning, the wind blowing snow across the highway
        and into the cattails
                just like the voice of God.
The last twenty miles behind a pulp truck, the logs with their new
        bark of snow
             just like the voice of God.

Like spaces between these lines, our lives filled in by her words.

If He was going to be like that,
she knew what to do.
Even when the words were lacking, she knew what to do.
From her black dress she would build a fire.
From her heart she would make a bellows.
A hammer from her elbow.
From her lungs tongs. And hammer out
the iron, hammer out the red hot iron
into a blade.
Let it cool with the coming of night. Sharpen
until it shined like the edge of morning.

Whatever you do, she said, you must use what is at hand.
Whatever you do, she said to us, you must use what is at hand.

Signe's Funeral

Her call was for each of us a long drive across snowy roads
      to a white frame church on a hill.
Those who lived near enough, who could get there,
      all turned to look as if it were God
arriving late.
The men with short hair, the women though they curled
      last night, their hair flattened thin by wool hats
now were ready for Him.
The minister too who thought he knew the words,
      which were flesh and which were God.
The angel from the high school who sang *Amazing Grace*
      in perfect pitch.
So few, we believed, would ever get there. Downstairs
      those who would
                  finding their heavy coats, accents
      saying how much they already miss her.
Have a sandwich. A piece of cake. A cup of coffee.
      There is Kool-Aid for the kids.

Grandmother, we miss you too. Pass the culture, please.

Heikki Goes America

This is why when I left Pohjanmaa
        I took *nisua* and coffee with my mother
        the way a man says goodbye before going to work.
This is why when in Michigan
        the day shift was the night shift and
a mile deep
        winter was even hotter than my dreams.
This is why deep down within the Quincy Shaft
        undercutting copper six days a weak-timbered week
        with barely enough air for a single candle
        I never forgot you. A Sunday marriage
                to whiskey or the church was never for me.
 I never even went to the Opera House with the other miners
        who spat down
                        on the smart suits of the bosses
and their velvet dressed wives
and were never seen. Someday I will come
with a gold ring and enough paper in my pocket
        to buy my property back.
I will ask you, and you will ask me
                                if I have been true.

I have,
I have.   I will never forget you.
                        Yours, Heikki.

P.S. Don't forget to make *nisua*.

Blacklist

1. The men's faces dropping one thousand feet per minute.
2. The dayshift in the mine.
3. The heavy seas of hematite.
4. The timbers creaking.
5. The Damp.
6. The air.
7. Lungs, of course.
8. The bosses chosen only for their tongues.
9. The blasting.
10. The undercutting.
11. When the canary doesn't sing and the minister does.
    How Great Thou Art.
12. The faces of the men on the lift.
13. Dark suits and dresses.
14. Widows and crows.
15. Tonnage.
16. And more tonnage.
17. Cave-ins.
18. Searches.
19. All the small money.
20. The men's faces in the negotiated-for bathhouse.
21. More blasting.
22. The men's faces in the Hall.
23. The ears that only hear red.
24. More money.
25. Alcohol.
26. Or the men without faces, their suits from Pittsburgh.
27. Silence.
28. Blood.
29. Not knowing if this is a life or not. And
30. the river between.

Board Feet

What they don't tell you is: the number of
thumbnails smashed purple, blisters
popping bleeding into
sweat-lined choppers, or their biceps
throbbing against the
frozen iron, back and forth
the toes curled up
in snowstuck boots, back and forth
the only rhythm like working and sleeping,
working and sleeping, the ears
ringing, ringing
as if wedges were hammered
in, ringing in
the sound now
like growth rings pacing out across the stump,
ear lobes frozen
and later the thaw stabbing through, but
for now
cheeks tingling, eyes looking up
and out
            for the splintering
beginning just before kick-
back when the smell of pine
                              remembers.

Now You Tell Me What You Believe

The coffin no longer than a violin case
              and on its stand
                            as if the musicians
just stepped outside to tell the others

that hell is always north, where they wanted to go
that they came to the new world because
              it was like the old world
that the Indians called them
              ones who were like them
that they were the first to build their homes from logs
that these lines I write look so much like those logs
that this is for those who know:

                        Ei siita seis puhua.

The Statue Of Liberty's Soliloquy

Give me your poor, your mouth breathing, your drooling.
Give me your tired masses.
I have floors to clean, tables to set, guests to feed.
       Give me preferably your Scandinavians.
I have shoes to shine. So hurry up now, give me
       your Blacks.
I have laundry. Give me a few Orientals.
I have flowers, lawns to trim, fruit trees. How about
       some Latinos.
I have boats to unload. Give me some Irish then.
I have minerals to mine. Give me any from the
       slag heaps of Europe.
I have this thin soil to till. So send me some serfs.
I have trees to cut. Finns will do.
Just give me your workers, your farmers. Give me your all.
I exclude no one—not even democrats. Socialists,
       communists, intellectuals excepted.
I have so much work to do.

The Politics of White

Below zero. When the wind slanted, the skin dried, and
        asphalt faded.
The warming trend. Snow falling.
The man's tracks leading north through birch trees,
        then westerly.
The feathers sticking to the tarred man.
The piece of paper without the words to explain.
The position not so much that you are for _____ as
        you are against _____.
Why you now waken in the night
        and see at last your own mother's teeth
in the exact spot

where a wolf turns and sneers, then disappears.

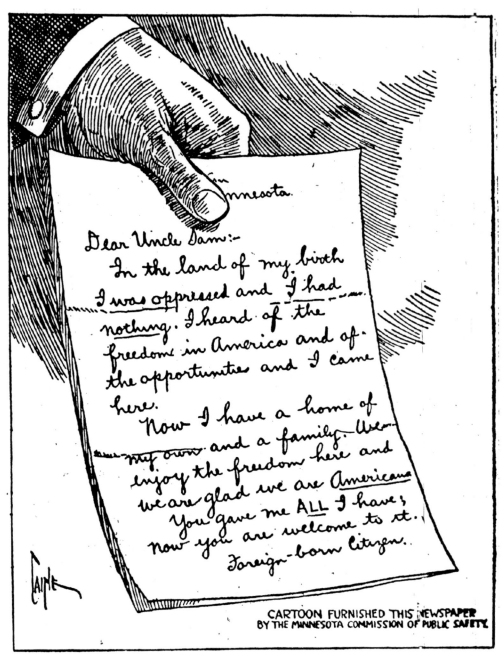

GENUINE LOYALTY

Headline **Carlton County Vidette** *March 29, 1918*

Unquestionably an organization exists to handle
disloyalty cases.

The Objects of the
Lincoln Loyalty League
are to enlighten its members in the duties and
rights of American citizenship, and to foster
unswerving loyalty to the United States.

1918

When he asked, Why you come here?
        he said, Cut trees.
When he asked, Miksi sina asuat boardinghouse-issa?
        he said, There was a man. One Olli Kinkkonen.
The day after he received his citizenship papers and
        swore under oath—afraid (this was in this country)
of the czar's army starving and under orders not to
        kill any of his pheasants—he returned them.
Then what did you do?

You would not have understood
        had you been there too.
The rope was not new, as if any old rope would do,
        as long as it was thick enough.
It was. Rough too. Somewhat worn,
        the frayed ends sticking out
like those cut bales he could have stood on, the pieces of
        clover, bird's foot, wild strawberry vine, and
popple twig sticking out, cutting into
        the inside of the wrist
hauling them from the fields, loading and
        unloading,
                        putting them out to feed.
This rope was the same, the same color even,
        left out too long in the rain.
All that fall.

The rope scratchy, not even tightened, but knotted
            behind his head.
The rope.
The other end hanging over the twisted branch
of the willow tree
leafless now. Here where it is low and not much of a creek
            all these branches are,
                              `   God bless them,
grown out everywhere and anywhere
            like the families of these men.
How little could they know. How little could they see.
Living their lives out
in shacks, shacks
            made of logs stuffed up with moss of
boards pieced together and nailed down with nails
            picked out of the ashes of other burned-down
shacks. Now
they too were just like those the wind had already weathered
            gray
as this willow you could not have understood
            if it were hanging over you
branching out everywhere and anywhere. And
above,
above all of this, the sky tightening up so tight
you just knew it had to snow. What then
            could these men know?
lucky enough to have any rope at all.

KNIGHTS OF LIBERTY TAR AND FEATHER SLACKER

Olli Kiukkonen Victim; Renounced Claim to Citizenship.

Six Others Sent Warnings to Be More Patriotic.

Olli Kiukkonen, who to make a long name short, has adopted the name of Olli Wirta since his residence in Duluth, is the first attendant at what may prove to be a series of tar and feather parties, which a body calling themselves "the Knights of Loyalty" have set out to apply to the six deliberate alien slackers who recently before local draft boards announced their desire to renounce claim to American citizenship rather than be inducted into the army. Each of the six had already taken out their first citizenship papers.

Kiukkonen, who boards with Charles Talonen at 227 South First avenue east, was called for at his lodgings last night about 10 o'clock, asked to show his registration card, and then invited to step into a waiting automobile. Headed for Congdon Park, the machine stopped while the following questions are said to have been put to him and the answers which he made were as follows, the information as to details being received by The Herald in a typewritten and unsigned letter this morning:

Questions and Answers.

"Do you believe in the Constitution of the United States and the justice of its war against the Central powers?" "Yes."

"How long have you been living in America and enjoying her prosperity and good wages?" "Ten years."

"Why did you take out your first papers?" No answer.

"Are you afraid to go in the army?" No answer.

Kiukkonen's answers far from satisfactory, they [decided] to tar and feather the offender [up to] this afternoon [he had not] reappeared at his [lodging].

[The following] questions as well as [the following] letter has been sent to each [of the six slackers] who are [listed: ...] West Eighth street, Superior, Wis.; Andus Hansen Seyford, 1116 Vernon street, Duluth; Theodore Johnson, 4 South Fifty-ninth avenue west, [...] Strom, 1109 Garfield avenue, [...] Hans Imbela, 217 South First [avenue] east, all of whom were reported by local draft boards as wanting to renounce their claims to citizenship.

"A Warning."

"The membership of the Knights of Loyalty numbers over 2,000,000 in America, and there are 75,000 members in the state of Minnesota. There are 5,000 members in St. Louis county and 2,000 members in the city of Duluth.

"These members are tried and true, sworn to protect and defend the Constitution of the United States of America and the Constitution of the Knights of Loyalty whatever the cost in blood, treasure and sacrifice.

"It is not our aim or purpose to persecute any free or loyal man, be he citizen or alien, enemy or friend, but without mercy, without fear and with a just relentlessness that will bring the coward and the guilty exponent of sabotage alike, be he citizen or alien, to his just deserts and brand him publicly before every true and loyal American and every loyal alien in his true light and in his craven colors, we shall, without malice, but with the fear of God in our hearts and with a sense of justice and righteousness, make it our aim and our commission to see that such parties enjoying the glorious freedom of the United States and its hospitality be given their full and just deserts.

"This is a part of the instrument of our oath of fealty, to organization, to principle, to conscience, to loyalty.

"Let every coward and slacker take notice. We will not be swerved in our duty to God, to our country and humanity.

"You have proven yourself a slacker. You have proven yourself an enemy of America. Let this be your warning and a warning to others of your caliber. The slacker cannot and must not exist in America. The slacker will not

---

TARRED ALIEN IS SUICIDE

Olli Kukkonen's Body Found Hanging Near Lester River Road.

Had Not Been Seen Since Punished By Knights of Loyalty.

The body of Olli Kukkonen, recent victim of a tar and feather party which took place after Kukkonen had renounced his claim to United States citizenship, in order to avoid being inducted into the army draft, was found hanging to a tree late yesterday by Arthur L. Fox, about a mile north of the Lester park pavilion and on the east side of the Lester River road. Circumstances point undoubtedly to suicide.

The body was found in a kneeling posture, a clothes line tied to a knot in a young birch tree being the means which Kukkonen had used to end his life. Fox, who has a cabin not 500 feet from where the body was found, and who passes there daily, had not noticed the victim of suicide until yesterday, and he at once notified the police. Chief McKercher, Detectives Lahti and Roberg, accompanied by Coroner James McAuliffe, arrived on the scene shortly before 6 o'clock, made a brief examination of the body, and determined that the man had evidently strangled himself, and had not been victimized for anything other than his alleged disloyalty.

Had Plenty of Money.

The Last Leaf

Actually, I cut it down, he said. I was the one.
When it thumped,
thumped against the ground,
I watched. Watched it longer than I ever watched
a life.
When it never moved, I went to take the boots.
First the one
and O! the smell.
Of tar and chickens. Shitted pants. Sweat. And
the soiled sock I ripped off
and there found a purple leg that ran into
a foot, a foot into toes and
Wait a moment! matted like a nest
there were 1-2-3-4-5
—10-15-20
—20 five-dollar bills stuck to the heel
I just had to kiss
and ripped off
the other boot so fast I never even
smelled what death had left. There
there were only 1-2-3
—20-21
—but what was wrong with that? 22 dollar bills.

What The Tamaracks Remember

That the ground around them, their needles fallen,
was then golden
while the white pines stood darkly by.

The Whip

Like dawn a crack in the dark night. In the earth. The heap
of clay frozen yet beside the crusted snow. When the banker
died, his name too was Winter, Frank said we should go to
town. I remember the words stood around useless like men
uncomfortable in pinstripes and thin ties. Words awkward at
moments like this. Words. What good could come from
words? Sheets were sheets folded up in dresser drawers.
Hoods with eyeholes merely ghosts. Names were nameless.
Faces faceless. It even snowed on Halloween as if to cover up
the earth. The whole town waiting until the thaw to plant his
body. Then there was the whip instead of flowers over the
grave. There were too the usual remnants—dented wash basin,
tire iron, rusted rim—blossoming in the spring.

Part Two:
The Co-op Label

Advice To A Young Wife

Look at those old photographs while I fix coffee.
I always spooned 42 ground beans into a granite
pot of boiling water, poured it out through a strainer,
into white china cups. Put absolutely nothing in it.
Saved my cream and sugar. Always believing a
proper cup of coffee would make my husband love
me.

Log House

I married him wanting to know of hewn wood.
I married him to know his fingers straight, straight
as every log he squared and every dovetailed
corner he fitted tight. The way he smelled of new
spruce and sweat that stained his plaid wool shirt
and bvds. Always wore those lumberjack boots
and stagged pants even in July. I married him
the way the sun shined through the cracks between
the logs that first year I thought would be forever.
The next year he built the new house with logs dried
out back. Though the trees he planted in the front
nothing but whips. How I remember that life.
Long log house. Every log straight. Front window
in line with the back window so I could see through
both. The fields behind. The trees trying to come
back at the edge where the field gave way to sand,
the sand to swamp. I married him to know he was
no farmer. And outlived him just to say so.

Black Spruce

Though I knew another, I won't say names—names must
be nameless—who built his house at the edge of the swamp.
His wife dead. I can see him with his three kids sitting
there thoughtless as those old shirts out on the line. Every
Sunday went to church. I suppose it was a good way to meet
a woman though no one ever told him babies shouldn't wear
black hats. His home well built. His corners tight. The logs
flat and flush. And good trim work around the windows.
But what kind of woman would live like that? Only the
weeds came up to his house. The trees standing in the
swamp so straight they must have been spruce. I ask you,
is there anything as straight as a black spruce, or as sad?

The Way Frank Loved Logs

Boards. Even sticks. Any wood hewn, planed, weathered
by wind or water. He could see the grain, however inexact
its history, how it curved, flowed around the knots like rocks
in the river, and knew how to work its fate into his. I could
not wait that way. When he finally came home from the
woods, I found in his pants a scrap of paper from Co-op
Motor: a receipt for $13.27 on the one side and, in his own
writing, *9:15 Thursday* on the other.

Green Turtle Soup

Chop the entrails, bones, coarse parts of the meat
    and put into a gallon of water with
    sweet herbs, onions, salt and pepper.
Cook slowly for hours in the shell of a
    dented aluminum pot.
In early June find them treading gravel, trying to cover
    their eggs as if preserving some dim romantic
    notion right there on the road, just before
    the turnoff onto the blacktop.
In the meantime, simmer the fine parts and green fat.
Thicken slightly with browned flour.
If there are eggs, boil them alone in clear water
    and add them to the soup.
Serve with cattail shoots, cranberry biscuits, and
    ice-cold buttermilk.

Location

This could be Kettle River, Iron River, Ironwood,
Floodwood. This could be Esko, Ely. Even
Embarrass. Could be Cloquet, Cokato, Calumet.
Why not Minot, New York Mills, or Harlem? This
could be the you-could-name-your-own-location
Farmers' Trading Co-op Company. This could be
why we came here: to be the same.

Hope On Parade

Of course all the girls wanted to be the queen just as
all the mothers wanted their daughters to be, but, you
see, there can be only one hope riding on the Farmers'
Union float in the Fourth of July parade in 1943.

At The Board Meetings

It was all written down. If one thought a manager should
be hired and another thought not. If one thought the
auditor's discretion was for the common good and another
thought not. If one recommended oats and another rye.
Though they agreed on grasshoppers. They agreed on
too much or too little rain. They agreed on Rudy. Rudy
who always wore a white shirt and black tie and became
the manager. And Rose who was the manager's wife.
They, too, were in the book. Though I must tell you
there were, at the time, two books. Now neither exist. I
am only telling you this because you asked and because I
want someone to know. I only remember because once
it was all written down. Twice.

When The New Manager Came

Rudy and Rose lived in that house at the end of the
Kohouma Road. I went there, said to visit. Tar paper
nailed down.   The roof unfinished. Around here you
need a roof, even though it rains so much you can't
seem to get enough time to nail one down. Rose had
already strung out the clothes line. She looked like
she was the one who was in charge. Her arms folded
across her chest. Her apron messed. A frown on her
face like it was a nuisance to have me there in the first
place, I suppose because the house wasn't finished yet.
Though she probably expected it would get done, even
with the crew she had. Grandpa bearded like some old
singer sitting on the porch, the tip of his cane between
his romeos. Did he think he would ever see it completed?
These things take more than a lifetime, though I knew
he'd lived long enough to know it didn't matter. And his
brother. I never did know what he was up to. While
Rose had her sleeves rolled up, he had on his winter coat
and two pairs of trousers. The rest were just boys
skinny as popple trees left uncut. Then I noticed,
above the tarpaper, two boards nailed to the corner
near the unfinished roof where the parrot was perched.
It was a frame house.

The Color of Eggs

That year 19 and 43 brought drought. We let our chickens
roam and they gave us brown eggs. The year so thin the
only grass the chickens found, inside the hops of
grasshoppers. Every yolk holding on to a trace of red.
Though I took that for a sign, I never told Frank. I had all
I could do to clean every egg with steel wool, sandpaper,
or emery cloth. Never washed them.

Rose And I Were Always Together

Walking a trail through the pines, the pines whispering
I suppose about Rose and I always together walking
toward a pond no one ever went to, too shallow for fish
to overwinter in, Rose and I always walking over a carpet
of moss, a carpet of green moss and flowers the Indians
called moccasin flowers, flowering, it was June, all around
us so pink now like flesh I told Rose the moss looked like
Frank's wool pants when he unzipped them and his flower
so pink pushing out and Rose and I laughing and laughing
until I asked Rose if Rudy didn't have that many zippers
and laughing again, though I couldn't imagine Rudy ever
unzipping those black pants he always wore, they never
had any kids, not while they lived in the county, yet Rose
and I, even after we couldn't see each other, were
always together, walking through the pines, the pines
whispering to each other how someone knew someone
who said to someone how someone knew someone. . .
and Rose said this would be our secret. I suppose she
meant the flowers.

Salting The Cows

Many nights I would be awakened by words, words
that had followed me out of my day.   I could not sleep
until I lit a candle and wrote. . .

>   In July the cows on pasture
>   do not forget
>   to salt them. Loose coarse salt is
>   preferable to rock salt.
>   Licking is a long slow process

. . . when I wrote that I imagined large audiences longing
for such detail. When I realized federal agents might be
my only audiences, I wrote in a more closed style.

Tomatoes

This co-operative never endorsed America's huge profit
business when it went all out for the war. In 1943
if you were to buy *tomatoes* in the store they would cost
8 cents per pound. We were naturally for America's
tomatoes because *tomatoes* gave us a chance to work
toward the economic democracy of the future. A
dictatorship that wants land for its survival must first
control the people's right to *tomatoes*.

When Frank Built The Addition

It was low and with not much of a pitch to the roof. In
the winter it was cold. I didn't really care, it was Frank's
house. I never went in there, except to clean. He put
in a woodstove. Not as tight as the main house. I
shouldn't have wondered. People all the time thinking
bigger and bigger. Did you ever dream you were
walking down one of those city streets, perhaps you
live there now, in the shadows of tall building after
tall building? You walk and you walk and you can't step
out of the shadows. That's what happened to us. The
chimney wouldn't draw when the wind came out of the
east and over the house, so he put in a taller chimney.
It was so tall the wind from the west blew it over. So he
nailed a tall pole to the side of the addition. The chimney
was nothing more than a stovepipe and the pole just west
enough to be a windbreak. He nailed another shorter
pole to the south side. He couldn't put wood against the
stovepipe and he needed it to be a stovepipe, he said,
otherwise he couldn't clean it out. Next to the pole he
leaned a ladder against the low roof stained black from
chimney smoke. Once you start these affairs they never
seem to turn out right. I don't know why. You could look
at our house and know what was was entirely haywire
here.

Where The Board Met

Out in the barn where the board of directors had to sit on
sacks of potatoes, old Kainulainen said, until they had dealt
with Musta the horse. Whether they felt the bumps or the
eyes that sprouted out of the gunny sacks were watching
them, they bought the truck. Whether or not the shadow
descended then from the grain dust down from the rafters
of the barn through the slanting light of the sun not one of
them would ever say.

When The Board Met

After that, on the first Saturday of the month if the
weather was rainy. If not, then on the next rainy day.
I remember it was the twentieth of July when the
board finally met. The meeting was in the afternoon,
Frank came home late and in the morning didn't want
to talk about it. Didn't want to talk about it. His loyalty
always before my health. After the war he even sent
25 dollars to striking miners in Mullen, Idaho. And
I left the sheets out on the line.

Everybody's Money

Our money was everybody's money. The till always
open. Some who cooperated more took less. Some
less who took more. When Rudy left town no one
would say more or less, only that we lost more and
more money. Except Frank who had more and more
to say about Rudy. After he forbad me to see Rose
I had less and less to say to him. Though I did notice
our prices rose. Businessmen in town took to meeting
after dark. The banker built a new bank. And I
considered more and more what the parrot had to say.

I
Believe
I
Will

have another cup of
this delicious coffee—

Red Star Coffee

with a fla

Carefully ple
Packed in vacuum cans to
wondrful flav

The Best You Ever Tasted

Why The Hammer And Sickle Appeared On A Co-op Coffee Can

He who knew the ways of steel fired the blade to yellow
     like the ripened wheat that sharpened the blade
     forever.
Even the generations removed across the sea, to a sea
     of grass, though the church decreed
     their names had changed,
made the handle fit the hand. Even there
when the sickle posed the question, the hammer answered.

Tomatoes Again

Here we grow our own. Here we planted the seeds in
milk cartons set out on a window sill in April. Here we
put the young plants into the ground in June. Then
we waited. If they made it through August without a
frost, they had a chance. There were those who took
them in, said they only turned red in the cellar, wrapped
in pages of the *Työmies*. Others preferred them green.
Once Frank built a frame around my garden, covered
it with glass, and brought tomatoes to the Co-op on the
sixth of July. That night boys threw rocks through all
those windows. Later broke all the stained glass in the
old church, too, so we knew it was just boys. Glass so
beautiful it would have been worth a fortune even then.

Predicting The Weather

Whether the sagging red belly of the sunrise meant rain.
Whether we should have voted for Henry Wallace or not
even bothered. Whether potatoes planted under the full
moon grew into the shape of your own soul. Whether Rudy
took our money. Though Frank said he knew. Whether he
knew my own moons had become irregular. An opportunity
Rudy couldn't refuse. Though we didn't know where. Why
we always waited until after the Fourth of July to cut hay.
Of course the board never admitted and I never considered
then what the parrot had to say. How do cows sleep?

Stone Harvest

You must not throw stones.
Stones are usable road material.
Stones must be picked if one is to improve
      the tilth of the land and
save machinery.
Be aware of their need for power.
They did not go away with the war.
Land farmed for 25 years, picked clean
      for 5,
yet we carried away another 8 ton of rock.

This was from my earlier work. I called it work even
though no good ever came from it. I believed in what
I was doing. It was my work once. Do you know,
solitary coffee drinker, now you are now my only
audience? Once, however, I had others.

Frank In The Back Of The House

Sitting in a rocking chair by the raspberries. His dog
Ressu blending into his shadow. They were my
raspberries. Frank built the alder fence around them.
He didn't want them there in the first place but built
the fence and never said. Liisa was just a girl. I can
still see her dress bleeding into that tree. Her stockings
slipped. I suppose she put that bow on herself. Now
she's married to a man who sells insurance. And Little
Frank with the bicycle he always brought out to show
everyone. Look at those clothes—white shirt, top button
too tight, black pants already too short—he outgrew them
so fast. I sent them then to the poor, a few copies of the
Työmies slipped in, instead of the *Bible*.

NIEMALA
NIEMELA
NIEMI
NIEMISTO
NIEMITALO
NIEMONEN
NIILEKSELA
NIKKA
VIKKILA
VIKKINEN
KULA
NKO
SKA

PARKKILA
PASANEN
PASONEN
PASSEJNA
PATOVISTI
PEILA
PEJKA
PEKKALA
PELKIE
PELKOLA
PELLI
PELLIKKA
PELLOSMA
PELLOSMAA

A List Of Names

I didn't know
      what the Heikkilas said about the Hovilas or
      what the Lumppios did in '23 after the Heinos
      married Hills and Kujawas sold cows to the
      Luomas and the Kurkkis joined the same church
      as the Siltonens and not the Alatalas. Maybe
      you know but
I didn't know.

A Knock At The Door

You never knew when the wind would come to the door
and knock, knock, knock all night long. In the morning
windblown snow already at the door. The linoleum cold.
The fire out. You never knew when the wind would get
under the door and knock, knock, knock all night long
like so many questions—Did you believe in the world in
the bud of a popple tree? Were any of the neighbors
watching tulips push out of the ground? Did you make
a list of first birds perched in the limbs of the mountain
ash? Send 25 cents to the Proletarec? Believe in
brotherly love? The wind wanted to know.

The Collected Works Of The Wife Of A
Co-operative Director/Farmer/Carpenter

It was the rain heavy on the metal roof of the hay
barn that sounded like the Underwood struck late
into the night. In the dim fringed light I listened
to a Vernon Dalhart record played and played. I
never longed for discussion at length. The new
world order became the old the moment the man,
smaller than I thought, pushed the red tinted
pince-nez to the bridge of his nose, looked at me,
and I thought better of my life. Now torn into many
pieces. I never read at the hall. I told him so.

What Happened To The History Of The Co-operative Movement

Nothing but poems. My life torn up into more pieces
than words. Stuffed between the logs of the house
like moss. Between pages of *The Egyptian*. Left
under the steps. In tins of flour. In cans buried in the
earth. Or folded, wedged into corners of the rafters
of the barn. Between bales of hay. In bins of feed.
Under stones placed carefully on the tops of fenceposts.
In rock piles. In the chicken house under the reliable
layers. Maybe the birds could use them. Maybe the
squirrels. For nest material maybe as good as it gets.

Joseph Stalin Pauses Among The Birches In Karelia

The moon steps out across the snow
and follows
the path between the birches
leading out into the lantern light where
Swedish newspapers
are spread across the sauna benches as if
they too were birches.
In this country too
straight white birches, birches straight as fingers,
fingers that press
the blade of the knife into the white outer bark and
cut a strip,
cut a long thin strip like a *kuperi* letting out
the blood
like it is yet another morning. The better ones never
left a scar.

Cupping

I remember the red blood blood red from the blue veins
like rivers flooding my grandmother's back. The red blood
curving from the knife slits in her sagging white skin. The
blood red. Like the Co-op label on every can. Almost
hammer and tempered sickle red. Red as a pike's gills.
Red as a chicken's comb, its head cut off. Red as fresh
meat. The pan under a slit pig. Sumac and maple leaf and
chain oil red. The eye of the loon. The door of the church.
The nose of the alcoholic *joulu pukki* coming in from the
cold and taking communion, drinking from the common cup.
Earth, fire, and iron ore. Red and more red. That was why
I washed my own skin with Fels Naphtha Soap. That was
why I laid out cow horns on the sauna bench. Cow horns
in all calibers. Cow horns to bring out the red. The red red
punainen red. My blood red blood. Red. Red. Redder
yet. Like the dawn's early red. When the straight edge of
the knife first cuts through the sky. Red. But not too red.

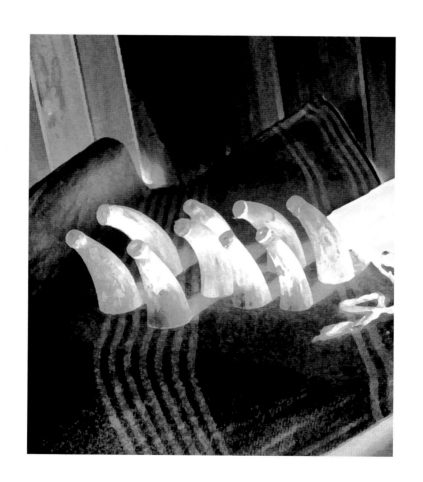

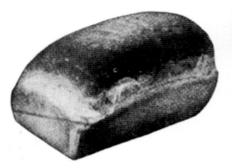

About Bread

I always used six eggs, two glasses of milk, more if
the eggs were small, four spoons of sugar, and stirred
with the flat wooden spoon, adding enough flour to
feel the knead just right. The old-fashioned way of
making a sponge is best. The compressed yeast of the
grocer is never the same, though some will tell you
Red Star is the yeast—the bread rising up, rising up like
bales in the fields, rising up like the workers' star in the
east. Do not listen to them. What could never happen
could never happen. Bread is what could be said. It is
not the body. Nor is yeast the soul. Bread is just bread.
I baked loaf after loaf for that old man and thought there
would be more.

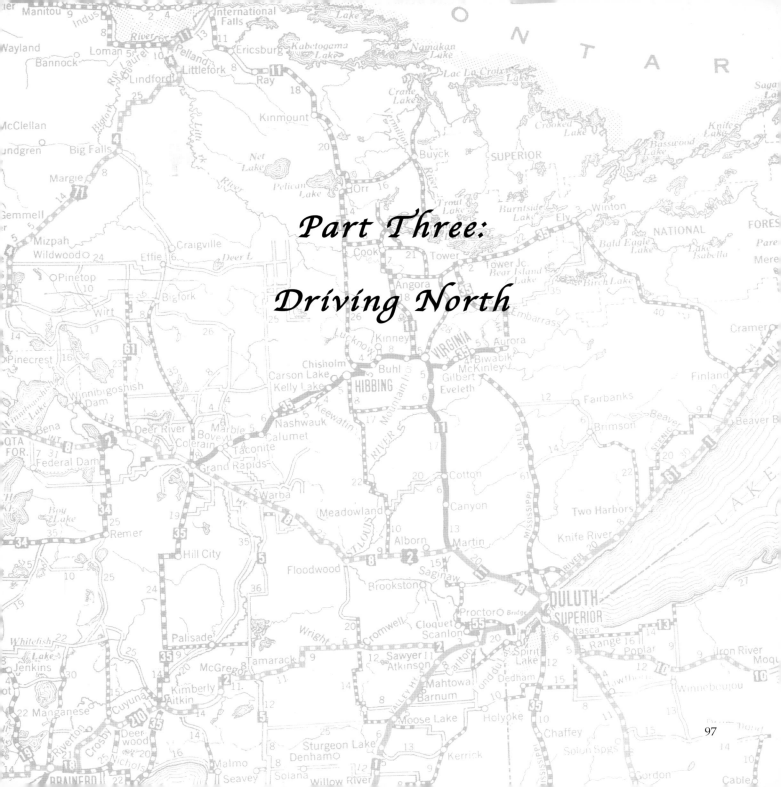

Part Three:

Driving North

Driving North

Driving north I see how
less and less
the spring has progressed.
More snow in the lowlands
or in the shadows of shapes.
Whiter the lakes.
No buds on the trees.
The roads puddled with mud;
the loggers laid off.
If you go far enough
into memory, on a rock face
the vermilion prints of human hands,
bears waking in the night
clawing the walls.
The return of the spirit to the body
is a difficult journey,
but the birds came anyway
long before the snow started to go.

Floodwood, Minnesota

Floodwood Minnesota is an Amoco Station/Little Store by the highway.
Floodwood Minnesota is the Stardust Motel the color of last year's cattails
    fading along the railroad grade.
Floodwood Minnesota is a grain elevator painted gray, the word *Co-op*,
    once so white, showing through.
Floodwood Minnesota is the Catfish Capital, says so on the water tower.
Floodwood Minnesota is a house without siding, only pink insulation board
    nailed down. In the yard piles of split wood. A corral without a horse.
Floodwood Minnesota is a blue-eyed dog.
Floodwood Minnesota is a man who welds, out back the young popple trees
    thick as his whiskers.
Floodwood Minnesota is a woman who bakes, talks on the phone. Her voice sagging
    like the lines strung from pole to pole knee-deep in a ditch.
Floodwood Minnesota is a girl who wears a red handkerchief for a scarf
    and picks blueberries all day.
Floodwood Minnesota is a boy who fishes for small trout, big pike.
Floodwood Minnesota is new potatoes, brown eggs, milk with cream on top.
Floodwood Minnesota is the angle at which birches walk over a hill.
Floodwood Minnesota is a new calf born in a blizzard or on the hottest day of summer.
Floodwood Minnesota is the howling of wolves.
Floodwood Minnesota is Viola Turpeinen's "Kulkarin Valsi."
Floodwood Minnesota is a place to speak: in a cafe, in an old hall, or
    on the bed of a pulp truck.
Floodwood Minnesota is a long walk into a bog.
Floodwood Minnesota is a compass that shows up or down,
    where you have been and where you are going.
Floodwood Minnesota is wire, duct tape, and binder twine—we can, we must fix everything.
Floodwood Minnesota is hard to find, like a pitch adjuster for an International mower.
Floodwood Minnesota is hard to lose. The pocket knife used by my
    one-armed grandfather. Once after I cleaned my fish
      I left it out on a rock.
In the morning I went back.

In July We Visit The Welder While The Iron Age Passes Us By

Too many black flies this time of year
and rainbow people.
A black cat purrs under the mower.
The sickle bar down, too many rocks.
The hay growing, too many flowers.
A flat tire on the John Deere now parked
under the only tree, it's 90 degrees, but
its shadow has long passed the tractor by.
In the barn by Menard
license plates nailed to the walls, bolts
in piles according to size, chains too
on respective nails.
While Ilmarinen
lights the torch and touches the rivets
one by one the blades clank down on the
concrete. The light itself
lingers in the rivets. This is how it is.
For a moment, we see
the tall trees, the lake in the half-life of
fireflies; they are welding
together the scraps of dark.
No thunder we had come to expect.
No trees, power lines down.
No hard rain. Instead all is calm.
But to get back to our lives
we must (at a dollar per bale if we get
the rain) not
invest too much
in machinery. Otherwise, why have horses?

In The Nursing Home, Ironwood, Michigan

The Finn has the kind of skin that
makes you think he knows
only of potatoes. Instead
he is an early version of the globe,
the continents his cheek bones,
the tears are ocean. It is the glare, he says,
that makes him squint. He has come from one
ruddy continent to another
where the petals of the wild rose fell to machinery
having come too late. Now
he cannot remember
what he ate
for dinner, if he even
waited his turn in line. How many years ago
was just the other day
when Billy Blacketter
and Clement Beargrease killed a bear,
a black bear,
a sow,
with a chainsaw. Flesh and blood dripped
from the popple buds, their limbs stuck with fur
like magnetic particles all pointed toward
the only North. So in this new world
the table is set: the plate, fork and knife and spoon,
but what are they for? Come to find out
history is a nursing home. His life
no longer a window. He must be thankful
just to be there
where there is no place to spit.

What A Radical Knows Of Potatoes

If you want to know, go now through the trap door.
If you want to know, go now down the slanting steps.
Go now into the cellar, now into the dark-timbered stone.
By bins and burlap sacks and shelves of glass jars
filled with eyes and jellies. Coils of snakes and wires.
Watch out for lead pipe and hard thought. But go.
Go now into the damp and spider-webbed corner.
Go now and see for yourself.
Sleeping in soft sand in a wooden crate.
Sprouted out, tangled in roots.
See for yourself. Eyes open in the dark.

What We Eat

1

in the country

Squash, four seeds and a fish head planted in hills.

Potatoes, seeds in rows planted in moonlight.

Beans, in a circle, a teepee of sticks.

Venison, early one morning by the gate a doe.

Northern pike, dark house, dark hole in the ice, the tines
        must break the surface before. . . .

Apple trees in the yard. Blueberries, new growth on
        sweet burned-over slopes.   Cranberries, high bush
        and tart.

Flour, butter, bitter coffee, sugar lumps, and cream
        at the Co-op (socialist, communist-type)—sold
        105 bales of hay, cedar logs after the freeze-up,
        56 jars of maple syrup.

No milk, only one cow.

As for eggs, mowed the neighbors fields. Always plenty,
what we eat. No insurance.

2

in the city

New potatoes, thin carrots, broccoli from the Farmers' Market.
        And apples if you don't have a tree.

Cheeses, wild rice, whole grains, black pepper, and allspice
        all from the Co-op (whole foods, hippie-type).

Herring from fishermen. Ask the butcher, Where?

What kind of feed?

Coffee from shops, Columbian, hazelnut, and blended
in beans.

Heavy breads and sweet, potica and cardamom.

As for milk, refuse the plastic teat.

And tomatoes, homegrown between the marigolds.

Build more houses. Sell more books. Teach school.
Take care of sick, the old.

It takes more than money. And no insurance.

What We Wear

Levis in Richmond, French Lick, and Lubbock.
Belts with big buckles in Albuquerque, in Paris.
Plain tee shirts with pockets in Fargo, Natichoches, and Newark.
Seed caps in Yankton, Peoria, and Columbus (you name your
own state).
Baseball caps Walt Whitman Mall in Long Island.
Bulls jackets in Blue Island.
Slouched hats in San Francisco, Hell's Half Acre.
Bolo ties in Alamagordo.
Blossom ties in Providence.
Vests with old suits in Floodwood.
Denim shirts in Kalamazoo and Butte.
Flannel shirts in Georgetown.
Button-downs in Boston, Charleston, and La Jolla.
Mainly plaids in Freeport.
Blazers in Kennebunkport.
Sport shirts in Savannah.
Long skirts in Santa Barbara, Coos Bay, and Amarillo.
Linens in Tuscaloosa, even Enid.
Coats from antique shops in Calumet, Gallop, and Galena.
Tweeds in Cambridge.
Shades in Vegas. Sunglasses in Jackson.
No socks in Huntington.
Sweat socks in Oxford. Rolled-down hose in El Paso.
Sponge curlers in Cloquet.
Parkas in Unalaska.
Long sleeves in the summers (because of the bugs)
in Skagway.
Down in Duluth.
Norwegian sweaters in Lake Wobegone and Vail.
North Stars jerseys in Dallas.

Boots in Big Timber, Poplar, and Aspen.
Moccasins in Bemidji and Minneapolis.
Sandals in Muskogee.
White bucks in Memphis.
Heels in Montgomery, New York City.
Hush Puppies in Lake Worth, in Tuba City, in Margaritaville.
Butt thongs in Salem.
Dashikis in Mount Vernon.
Scarves in Beverly Hills, Salt Lake, and Selma.
Silk and lace in Toledo.
Tights in Williamsburg.
Turquoise in Tucumcari.
Khakis in Lead. Chinos in Gary.
Leather in Sturgis.
Bellbottoms in Berkeley. Bandannas in Watts.
Tattoos in New Orleans. Beads in Berea.
Sequins in Nashville, Mukilteo, and Miami.
And please, as this poem wasn't written in Taiwan,
no polyester in Sedro Wooley.

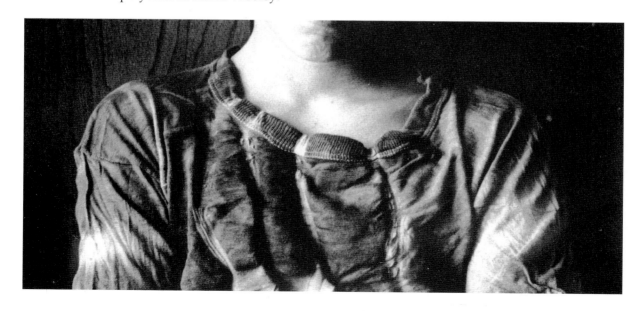

What We Believe

Now that the field is cut
the suburbs grow out like petals of a daisy,

not like the beautiful paw marks of capitalism.

In Praise Of Lutefisk

In late November he dipped the slabs—whitefish,
        sucker, or burbot—
in lye and stockpiled them out back along the shed
        like stovewood.
                Frozen, snow-covered
each slab he sold he chopped out of its own ice.
That dogs pissed on them didn't seem to affect
        the flavor.
The smell that steamed the windows of every Christmas Eve
        preserved his life
                and ours—salted, canned
like meat, dried like flowers, distilled like night. In coffee cans,
        cookie jars, tin boxes
buried out in the orchard. Mattresses stuffed. Bank accounts.
Much less could be said
              that he invested wisely in lutefisk.

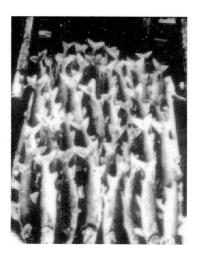

County Road 7, St. Louis County, Cherry Minnesota, U.S.A.: Posthumous Interview With Gus Hall

My name *Ja ja,* is Gus Hall, born Arvo Kusta Halberg
in a log house
here in the North where the land *Ja* flat and poor,
my father in the union so out of work,
I read books, worked the lumbercamps,
went first
the Lenin Institute, then *Ja, ja* straight to Leavenworth.
I won't tell you how uncomfortable
it was *Ja, ja* to finally organize and run
legally for president. I will tell you

Ja, ja I have spoken from dynamite
boxes in the mines, from the beds
of pulp trucks and hay wagons, small town
street corners, stages in dark halls, as well as big
city sidewalks and parks, flash-bulb
breaking, red-white-and-blue creped
conventions.
Where there were those *Ja, ja* who even wrote down
my words. Not so easy. *Ja, ja, ja*
I talked and talked. Though you should know
what could not be said. I had my ideas
Ja, ja, ja as you have yours. Thank you for not saying.

How flat these fields once farmed *Ja, ja* only for hay,
now gone back to pulp wood. As a little traveler
you should know
once stopping
along a county road was *Ja, ja* to invite many opinions.
Maybe this is how we met. When the tractor missed
I listened *Ja, ja* instead
to a screwdriver
the handle to my ear, blade to the block. Suppose it said,
Tappets. Then
into the barn where the same screwdriver, *Ja* a steady
hand *Ja, ja* and flashlight worked on
into the dark.

It was not so long ago when I awoke
to find purring at long last
Asso,
the black cat, asleep on my chest. Know then
this *Ja* is true democracy.

Lenin's Death Day

All were welcome at the hall.

On Saturday nights after the speeches there were dances.
Yet when Lenin's Death Day fell on a Saturday, John
Mikkola announced, *Tonight there will be no dancing.*
John Mikkola, who was a big man, looked sternly about,
buttoned up his mackinaw, pulled up his collar, and buckled
his five-buckle overshoes. Then John Mikkola opened
the door. The cold, the snow, the sound of the wind blew
in. For a moment. Then he was gone.

Everyone sat. For the longest time no one moved. No
one knew what to do. When one man picked up the fiddle
case and set it on his knees, thinking, another man reached
for the accordion, wondering. The man with the fiddle
began tapping the case. Another man reached for a guitar,
as if to ask, *What if?* Soon these men found themselves
walking to the stage. Benches pushed to the back and to
the sides. Coats and sleeping children piled on the benches
in the back of the hall.

Near the front and on the side sat the old women. Like a
jury, the old women looked out onto the middle of the
floor where one couple, then another couple, and yet
another began to dance to the old world rhythm. Era after
era. Strata after strata. Each couple dancing, dancing in
a new world, a world revolving now around its mother,
stern and old, yet needing something to talk about, now
that the father had finally gone to bed.

County Roads, Deer Trails, And Crows

In Lake County where deer trails only recently
            gave way to roads,
someone drives. The light rain that has
            been falling stops
and the sun drives a wedge to open the sky
            to fir trees and fields.
Soon it will be dusk and the gravel will give way
            to blacktop.

Once as I drove County 4, a deer, antlers in velvet,
            running along the side—my foot
off the gas pedal, my mind already on the brakes—turned,
crashing into the side of the truck.
I stopped.
Looked at the deer,
belly on blacktop, legs struggling but not splintered
            or broken. No blood.
It got up, wobbly at first, as if newborn
            as indeed it was,
and somehow became the alder across the road.

Now with the coming of dusk the road seems longer
            than life.
The brown needles of the dead fir tree reincarnate
            a deer in its June fur.
The humus clinging to an uprooted tamarack
            resurrects the legs and antlers of a moose.
The clump of sod gets up a porcupine.

Nothing ever dies.
One thing gives way to another and becomes
          its shadow
Day flows into night. The body crosses over
          and becomes the soul.

That

That these poems are meant to be read in an old hall. That
the hall was once a hunting camp. Or a union hall. That now
it is low-ceilinged. With dark wainscoted walls. A rough-sawn
stage in one corner. Lit by a single stained-glass lamp. Or a
lantern. That the sun has set. That music will follow. Perhaps
dancing. But first coffee and Kool-Aid will be served. Along
with cake. That questions will be asked. Answers debated.
Then more cake, more talk. That some may step outside for
more spirited discussion. Or to pee in the woods. Look up at
the stars. And know. We are connected, truly connected, to
this world.

Notes To The Poems

Viilia—A culture, in Finnish. When I was growing up, I thought culture was something that grew in a jar in the refrigerator where my father grew *viilia*. I was told it had begun long ago in the old country.
Also, thanks to Judy Bonnovetz and ancestors for their old photographs and olive oil.

Huivi/Huivit—Scarf, scarves. *Huivis*, plural in Finglish. Usually dark scarves that women wore over their heads and wrapped around their necks. Often only their noses stuck out like beaks.
"At Kaleva Hall" is for Dave Kess.

In 1917 the Finnish Civil War was fought between the Whites, supported by Germany, and the Reds, supported by Russia. In America these elements didn't always melt down as easily as some would have believed.

Pohjanmaa—North land. An area in Finland.

Nisua—The old Finnish word (The modern Finnish word is *pullaa*.) for cardamom biscuit. *Nisua*, once meaning wheat, also has a Biblical connotation and is still used in some areas of Finnish-America but not in Finland. Old words hide out in the strangest of places.

Ei siita seis puhua—Of these things we do not speak. In our family you knew these were the important things.

Miksi sina asuat boardinghouse-issa?—Why did you live in a boardinghouse? Olli Kinkkonen was lynched for returning his citizenship papers after the *vanhatpohjat* (bachelors, old boys in Finnish) told him, jokingly I presume, that as a citizen he could be drafted.

The Co-op Label—Many of the poems in this section were inspired by the January and July, 1943, issues of *The Co-operative Builder*.

Työmies Eteenpäin—Finnish language communist newspaper. In Minnesota the Communist party financially helped the Co-ops set up their own wholesalers at a time when the big suppliers were trying to drive them out of business. Later the Communist Party asked the Co-ops to return the favor, but the Co-ops refused, stating that their charter did not allow them to be political.

Cupping was done by a *kuperi*.

Joulu Pukki—Santa Claus. *Punainen*—red.

The phrase "the beautiful pawmarks of capitalism" is from Pentti Saarikoski.

"Lenin's Death Day" is from the oral history of Bill Johnson.

The following letter is from *The Co-operative Builder*:

Open Letter To Wisconsin Congressmen

Honorable Alexander Wiley, Honorable Joseph R. McCarthy,
Honorable Alvin E. O'Konski, Honorable Merlin Hull

Dear Wisconsin Members of the United States Congress:

As our name indicates we are a cooperative association of farmers. We have 557 members and have been serving our people, without profit, since our incorporation in 1914. As a law-abiding, tax-paying, Wisconsin corporation we necessarily appeal to you to exert your influence even more, on the floor of the Congress, and elsewhere to counteract that well-greased, highly-financed, brazenly-lying propaganda of the National Tax Equity League that we don't pay taxes. We pay every tax that has been levied and gladly so. We want no handouts and receive none.

They picture us as un-American. To be an American is to be democratic in both spirit and practice. We are as thoroly American as anyone. We take our democracy seriously and put it into freest practice both as citizens of the United States of America and as members of our cooperative association. Our patriotism is unchallenged.

Person for person the cooperative folk outnumber those who constitute the NTEA. Dollar for dollar, however, we cannot hope to match their propaganda funds. Altho we are many in number, our people are of a limited financial means. On the other hand, the NTEA represents wealth, much of it no doubt ill-gotten. With their filthy dollars they are out to wreck these many vitally-necessary, democratic, nonprofit enterprises of the masses of plain Americans. It boils down to a choice between soulless dollars on the one hand and human beings on the other.

As our Wisconsin representatives in Congress we are a necessarily counting on you to choose the side of human beings, as against the NTEA dollars, and to do so not only by voting right yourselves, but in seeing that others vote right.

Your personally aggressive leadership is needed in this fight. We want you there in the limelight, with your sleeves rolled up, fighting for the truth and for the people and their cooperatives. The responsibility is clearly yours to prevent the passage of laws that would tax cooperative patronage refunds, which taxes would be brazenly discriminatory and punitive and un-American.

Respectfully yours,
Arnold J. Ronn, General Manager
Maple Farmers' Cooperative
Maple, Wisconsin
August 9, 1951

Notes on the Images

These images were taken, scavenged, found, located, scanned, manipulated, combined, and reconstituted to form glimpses of truth and fragments of fiction. All photos are taken by or are from the collection of Marlene Wisuri unless otherwise indicated. Other photographers or photo studios are credited when known. Unknown photographers are indicated by unkn.

title page - photo Marlene Wisuri

6 - unkn

7 - photos clockwise from upper left corner, Nummi, C. N. Johnson, unkn, Westberg

8 - photos clockwise from upper left corner, C. E. Larson, Stafford, unkn, Wilhelm Riege, Harrison's Studio, unkn, center photo R. A. Cowan

10 - photo Marlene Wisuri, unkn

13 - unkn

14 - photo Marlene Wisuri, unkn

16 - unkn

17 - unkn

18 - photo Marlene Wisuri, unkn

20 - collection Carlton County Historical Society

21 - collection Carlton County Historical Society

22 - A. M. Turnquist

24 - photos clockwise from upper left corner Chaney, unkn, Octavie Morneau, unkn, unkn, Dempsie Minnette Photos, Dorge, Dempsie, S. Sandstrom, unkn, Eveleth Photo Studio, J. H. Carlisle, center photos unkn, A. Gozanski, Oleson

26 - photo Marlene Wisuri

28 - *Carlton County Vidette*

29 - collection Carlton County Historical Society

31 - photo Marlene Wisuri

32 - *The Duluth Herald*, September 19, 1918, *The Duluth Herald*, October 1, 1918.

33 - photo Marlene Wisuri

34 - photo Marlene Wisuri

36 - photo Marlene Wisuri

38 - collection Carlton County Historical Society

39 - collection Carlton County Historical Society

40 - J. C. Hendricks

43 - J. C. Hendricks

44 - J. C. Hendricks

46 - photo Marlene Wisuri

47 - unkn

48 - collection Carlton County Historical Society

52 - collection of Sue Raker

54 - M. Mathieson

57 - J. C. Hendricks

58 - photo Marlene Wisuri

60 - unkn

62 - photo Marlene Wisuri

64 - photo Marlene Wisuri

67 - J. C. Hendricks

69 - photo Marlene Wisuri

70 - unkn

72 - unkn

74 - photo Marlene Wisuri, *Co-operative Pyramid Builder*

77 - photo Marlene Wisuri

78 - photo Marlene Wisuri

80 - J. C. Hendricks

82 - photos Marlene Wisuri

84 - photo Marlene Wisuri

87 - unkn

88 - photo Marlene Wisuri

90 - photo Marlene Wisuri

93 - photo Marlene Wisuri

94 - *Co-operative Pyramid Builder*

96 - unkn

97 - Official road map of Minnesota, 1927

98 - photos Marlene Wisuri

100 - photo Marlene Wisuri

101 - photo Marlene Wisuri

102 - unkn

104 - unkn

106 - photo Marlene Wisuri

109 - photo J. C. Hendricks

111 - photo Marlene Wisuri

113 - photo Marlene Wisuri

114 - collection Carlton County Historical Society

115 - unkn

116 - collection of Iron Range Research Center

118 - collection of Iron Range Research Center

121 - unkn

122 - collection of Iron Range Research Center

127 - photo Kathryn Nordstrom

128 - photo Marlene Wisuri